The **D**iscipleship **S**eries

Other titles in the series

5

Insights to Discovering Your Place in the **Body of Christ**

Published by CWR, Waverley Abbey House,
Waverley Lane, Farnham, Surrey GU9 8EP, England.

Copyright © 2001 by Selwyn Hughes
First published in Great Britain 1982
ISBN 1 85345 175 4

Typesetting: Start
Printed in Finland by WS Bookwell
Illustrations: Helen Reason
Front cover image: Helen Reason

5

Insights to Discovering Your Place in the Body of Christ

Selwyn Hughes

Contents

Preface

Prior to entering the Christian ministry I heard an elderly preacher say that that everyone has a problem, is a problem or lives with a problem. At first I was a bit sceptical of that statement but no sooner had I entered the ministry than I found those words to be true. Problems of all shapes and sizes were brought to me and, feeling ill-equipped to deal with them (my Bible College training taught me a lot about God but little about people), I went to the United States for training in the area of biblical counselling. How glad I am that I took time out from my work as a pastor to focus on discovering the biblical causes that lie beneath human problems and how to utilise the truths of Scripture in correcting them.

The booklets in the Discipleship Series set out to confront some of the difficulties or issues that Christians come up against when seeking to live as Christ's tenty-first-century disciples. They are written with two groups of people in mind. Firstly, those who are looking for something that will speak clearly and concisely to their present need and secondly, those, such as counsellors or ministers who want to offer some additional material to people they are seeking to help that will supplement their own individual counselling efforts.

My prayer is that God will make these brief but prayerfully written booklets a blessing to those who seek to become Christ's true and faithful disciples.

Selwyn Hughes

What is the **Church?**

"I just don't know what to do. I've been a Christian for less than a year and I've been given a job in my church which is getting me down. Everyone thinks I am well fitted for the task they have given me but I know deep down in my heart it is not the place God has for me. I'm afraid I will have to give up going to church unless someone tries to understand my problem and help me."

Brian, a 25-year-old accountant, came for counselling because he had been assigned a task by the officials of his local church which he felt was not in line with his basic spiritual abilities. As a result he was experiencing a good deal of anxiety and frustration. After several hours of counselling, during which he was shown how to discover and develop his basic spiritual gift, he returned to his church and suggested to his minister that he be given a task more in harmony with the basic gifts God had given him. After long discussion with the minister and the elders, when Brian was able to share the results of his counselling session with me, he convinced the church leadership that the role they expected him to play in the growth of the church was incompatible with his natural spiritual abilities. Brian was then given a new task: one more in harmony with his basic gifts and which gave him a great degree of spiritual fulfilment.

The minister of the church, when writing to me a little later concerning Brian's situation, said, "We have decided to approach every member of our church in a much more cautious and prayerful manner than we have previously done so that we help them to discover, not what we want them to be doing but rather what are God's purposes for their lives in this part of His Body, the Church."

How sad it is that in many churches people are assigned tasks for which they are not fitted either by natural or spiritual endowment and they become, so to speak, like square pegs in round holes. The subject of discovering our proper place in the Body of Christ, although well understood and practised by the Early Church, is greatly neglected by Christians at the start of the twenty-first century. It is my conviction that Christians who discover and develop their basic spiritual gift will function in the Body of Christ with *maximum effectiveness* and *minimum weariness*. If they fail to discover the place God wants them to fulfil and try to undertake a task for which they are not divinely fitted, then they will function in that role with *minimum effectiveness* and *maximum weariness*.

Paul, the great planter and builder of New Testament churches took care to teach his converts the principle of discovering their basic gifts as one of life's priorities. His desire for every newly formed church was that they might develop their ministries in harmony with God's personal plan for their lives. Take, for example, the situation in the New Testament churches mentioned in Acts 14:1–18. These churches, being newly formed, had no members mature enough to qualify as elders or deacons but, thrown on the inner resources provided by the Holy Spirit, no doubt they put into practice Paul's teaching on the discovery and development of their gifts so that within a comparatively short time the members had matured enough for some to be chosen as elders on Paul's return visit (see Acts 14:21–23). You see, in every congregation of God's people the basic gifts needed for the development and maturity of that group are already deposited there by God. The task left to us is to discover these gifts, develop them and use them in the way God desires.

Before we can begin to discover and develop our basic spiritual abilities, however, we must first have some insight into the *nature* of Christ's Church. As a first-hand observer of the spiritual life of the Church for over 50 years, I have come to the conclusion that the Christian Church is suffering from an identity crisis. It's like an amnesia victim trying to find out, "Who am I?". We are divided by so many different ideas, doctrines and denominations that we are in danger of losing our proper spiritual identity.

What then is the Church of Jesus Christ? Is it something tall and Gothic, with beautiful architecture and stained glass windows? No, that is the house in which the Church worships. The Church is people – born-again people. They may meet in a cathedral or in a cottage; a magnificent complex, or an ordinary house; but the building is relatively unimportant. "The Church" said someone, "is a farmer ploughing in the field, a housewife at the kitchen sink, a mechanic in a garage, a student in a classroom. Wherever there is a heart that is redeemed by the Blood of Jesus Christ, there the Church exists."

The Apostle Paul's favourite analogy of the Church, in both Corinthians and Ephesians, is the body. It throbs with life: Jesus Christ is its head and you and I, as believers, are its members. The members are gifted to function as an organism and they have a rich fellowship with one another. Every single believer is like a living cell in that body, and for the body to function effectively every cell must live in harmony with all the other cells.

Wherever a group of those living cells of Christ's Body meet to organise themselves into a community for fellowship and spiritual enrichment, there a local church exists. The New Testament gives specific instructions on how a local church should function and pays a good deal of attention to the principles underlying the corporate functioning of such a group of God's people. The question is often asked, however: "What defines a local church? When does a group of God's people meeting together become a church?"

Throughout history many have tried to define what constitutes a local church and their efforts have served us well. The Reformers, for instance, gave the following definition: "The Church exists where the Word of God is preached and where the sacraments of Baptism and Holy Communion are faithfully administered: to the end that men would come to faith in Christ." Some of the Reformers also included a statement that the exercise of church discipline was necessary in order for a local church to be a bona fide part of the Body of Christ.

Rome countered this definition with one of her own which is roughly as follows: "The Church is made up of the faithful baptised who receive the sacraments under the government of the priesthood who, in turn, are under the authority of one visible head on earth." Others have attempted to define the Church in terms of style of living and code of behaviour. Some local churches define believers in terms of specific things they do or specific things they don't do rather than their relationship with God. If you tithe you are a true believer; if you don't then you are not. I know one church where those who wear jewellery are regarded as heathen. The officials of another church I was in some years ago told me that no one was regarded as a true believer unless he or she had spoken in other tongues. How refreshing it is to turn to Scripture and read, "Nevertheless, God's solid foundation stands firm, sealed with this inscription: 'The Lord knows those who are his'" (2 Timothy 2:19).

Francis Schaeffer indicated seven ingredients which he claimed must be part of "the policy of the church as a church":

1. Local congregations made up of Christians.

2. Special meetings on the first day of the week.

3. Church officers (elders) who have responsibility for the local churches.

4. Deacons responsible for the community of the church in the area of material things.

5. A serious view of church discipline.

6. Specific qualifications for elders and deacons.

7. The observance of two sacraments, baptism and the Lord's Supper.

A good deal could be written on the subject of the nature of the universal Church and the local church but that is not the primary purpose of this book.

The way I would answer the question, "What constitutes a local church?", is like this: "A local church exists whenever a company of believers meet together around the Word of God, submit to its authority and are organised under the leadership of a properly constituted governing body that exercises Scriptural disciplines and control to the end of bringing Christians to maturity and non-Christians into a personal relationship with Jesus Christ." This I believe to be the irreducible *minimum* for a local church run on New Testament principles.

In order for a local church to develop spiritual maturity all of its members must function in the way God designed them. Paul puts it like this: "Here is what I am trying to say: all of you together are the one body of Christ and each one of you is a separate and necessary part of it" (1 Corinthians 12:27, TLB). As in the human body each part is designed to function in harmony and interdependence, so are we positioned in Christ's Body to perform a specific and God-designed task. *Performing that task to the fullest possible degree is the main calling of every Christian.*

It becomes clear when we read the New Testament that God does not expect any believer to live in isolation. In Matthew 18:19 Jesus said that if two Christians agree on earth concerning anything they ask, his Father in heaven will do it. He went on to say (verse 20), "For where two or three gather together because they are mine, I will be right there among them" (TLB). Paul, writing to the Romans says, "Just as there are many parts to our bodies, so it is with Christ's body. We are all parts of it, and it takes every one of us to make it complete, for we each have different work to do. So we belong to each other, and each needs all the others" (Romans 12:4–5, TLB).

For Christ's Body to be in perfect health all of its members must function as they have been designed. Each believer must see that he or she is in the Body, not primarily to express themselves but to build up the Body. A cancerous cell, so I am told, is one that ceases to be contributive and seeks not to minister, but to be ministered unto. Once a cell in our bodies ceases to become contributive then it can become cancerous. Once we understand that our place in Christ's Body is to minister to the needs of others and not to get others to minister to our needs we are on the way to true fulfilment, for fulfilment comes not through getting but through giving.

One of the reasons for frustration amongst believers arises from the fact that they do not know precisely what it is God has fitted them to do in His Body. Joy comes when we discover our place in the Body of Christ, fit into the perfect pattern that God has prepared for us and contribute to the functioning of Christ's Church according to God's design. Every Christian has at least one basic gift. You may feel very inept and inadequate but, believe me, God has gifted you to do at least one thing well in the community of believers we call the Church. So congratulations – you're gifted! Sometimes ministers unwittingly curb the development of gifts within a congregation when they play the "I've-got-to-do-everything" role. Where this happens spiritual gifts lie dormant in the lives of those who form that particular congregation, when really they should be taking an active part in the ministries of teaching, counselling, etc. The frozen assets of the Church will never be thawed out until we put into practice the biblical doctrine of discovering our basic gifts. Then, and only then, will unemployment be rooted out from amongst God's people and the universal priesthood of all believers truly realised.

2

Basic gifts –
gifts we have

The New Testament introduces us to three distinct streams of gifts which are listed respectively in Romans 12:6–8, 1 Corinthians 12:8–10 and Ephesians 4:11–12. After studying these passages for a number of years now it is my belief that each member of the Trinity assumes responsibility for the administration and operation of a particular set of gifts. In Ephesians 4:11–12 the gifts there are described as coming under the direct control of our Lord Jesus Christ: in other words they are Christ's gifts to His Church. In 1 Corinthians 12:8–10 the gifts are said to be under the control and administration of the Holy Spirit. In Romans 12:6–8, although there is no specific reference to these gifts coming under the direct control and administration of the Father, I believe it safe to assume, on the basis of what I have said, and considering the precise nature of these gifts, that they are distributed and administered by God the Father. The gifts outlined in Romans 12 for the purpose of this study will be described as "basic gifts".

Before we begin to examine the first list of gifts in detail and gain an insight into their purpose and how they function, we must pause to clarify the difference between a basic gift and a talent. Simply defined, a basic gift is a spiritual motivation or an inward drive within our personalities which prompts us to minister in certain directions within the Body of Christ. A talent is a natural aptitude to do something well, such as an ability to paint, to sing, to write, to speak, and so on.

According to the Scriptures, before we were born, God's sovereignty was at work preparing us for our emergence into this world. The Psalmist said, "You were there while I was being formed in utter seclusion! You saw me before I was born and scheduled each day of my life before I began to breathe. Every day was recorded in your Book" (Psalm 139:15–16, TLB). God shaped Jeremiah for his ministry saying to him, "Before I formed you in the womb I knew you, and before you were born I set you apart" (Jeremiah 1:5). According to these and other scriptures (see Luke 1:16, Galatians 1:15) a Sovereign God is at work preparing us to contribute to His universe in certain well-defined ways. In each one of us God builds into our personalities at the moment of conception (so I believe) certain aptitudes and abilities which later, through growth and development, become observable. Once we become Christians, however, a spiritual transformation takes place in which the Holy Spirit regenerates our dead human spirits (see Ephesians 2:1) and brings us to new life and a new identity. Immediately we are converted at least one of our basic abilities (sometimes more than one) is harnessed by the Holy Spirit to become our specific contribution to the ministry of development in Christ's Body, the Church. There takes place within us, whether we feel it or not, an inner thrust, or if you like, a distinct motivation, which leads us towards a specific form of ministry in Christ's Body. This inner drive is what constitutes a basic gift. It is the heightening and intensification, or as some prefer to call it, the "Christianising" of a natural ability in such a way that an individual finds himself or herself inwardly motivated to play a certain part in building up the Church.

A basic gift then is a spiritual urge or motivation, produced by the Holy Spirit, alighting and impinging on a natural ability so as to sanctify it, and transfigure it so that it becomes the potential for a significant contribution in the ministry of the Church. It does not mean that every natural ability is taken up by God in this way but one, at least, most certainly is, enabling believers to play their part in the most wonderful ministry in the universe – maintaining the health and vitality of Christ's Church here on earth.

It is my belief that every Christian has at least one basic gift and is specifically called by God to contribute to His Church in a certain way. Without that gift then no positive contribution can be made to Christ's Body because the Church is a spiritual organism, not a natural one, and requires, for its growth and enlargement, a spiritual input. In order to be able to gain an insight into what part we are designed to play in Christ's Body, we must examine the set of gifts described in Romans 12 in detail: "Through the grace of God we have different gifts. If our gift is preaching, let us preach to the limit of our vision. If it is serving others let us concentrate on our service; if it is teaching let us give all we have to our teaching; and if our gift be the stimulating of the faith of others let us set ourselves to it. Let the man who is called to give, give freely; let the man who wields authority think of his responsibility; and let the man who feels sympathy for his fellows act cheerfully" (J. B. Phillips). The reason I am using the J.B. Phillips translation here is because I believe some of the words he uses (like preaching, stimulating the faith of others, wielding authority, sympathy) give a clearer indication of what the original Greek is saying.

It can be seen from this that there are seven specific gifts mentioned here:

1. *Preaching:* The Greek word used here is *propheteia* which means public exposition or presenting truth with force, clarity and conviction. Some translations use the word "prophecy" here but this use of the word is not the same as the gift of prophecy spoken of in 1 Corinthians 12, or the office of a

prophet as described in Ephesians 4:11. It is the gift of inspired preaching; the God-given ability to present truth in such a way that it touches the conscience of the hearers and exposes unrighteous motives.

2. *Serving:* This is a gift which enables the recipient to be extremely sensitive to the personal needs of others. A person who has this gift will demonstrate a deep concern and desire to help another brother or sister in practical ways so that they can be freed for greater and more effective service. Such a person will also overlook personal comfort and convenience so that the needs of others can be met.

3. *Teaching:* This gift enables the one who possesses it to clarify biblical truth with great effectiveness. Such a person will find within himself a deep desire to search out and validate truth, dig around for important facts, manifest great diligence in study and compare one Scripture with another so that the truth can be presented in a proper perspective.

4. *Stimulating the faith of others:* This, I, believe, is the gift of personal counselling. Some people in Christ's Body are gifted with spiritual eagerness to help others with their problems. Whenever they see a weak or lame Christian something rises within them to respond by personal encouragement and counselling. They have that special ability to come alongside a struggling believer, to say the right words and to minister to them in such a way that helps them resolve their problems.

5. *Giving:* A person with this gift will manifest a high degree of wisdom in relation to material giving. Such a person will show skill in organising their personal affairs and assets so as to be able to enrich the work of God in material ways. The gift carries within it a God-given wisdom to make quick and sound decisions about the right use of money.

6. *Wielding authority:* A person with this gift will show a great ability to preside over the activities of others and be able to co-ordinate other people's labour and activities towards the best advantage. Such a person will not only be able to look ahead and distinguish major objectives for the group or the community, but will also have the ability to clarify them for others.

7. *Sympathy:* This gift enables a person to demonstrate a deep sympathy and empathic understanding towards the misfortune of others. Such a person will find it easy to enter into the emotional needs of others and relate to them in a helpful way. There will be a warmth flowing from them that can bring healing to the one who is downcast, without any words being spoken.

Someone has described these gifts as "an inward drive which comes to life at conversion by which we contribute to the health and growth of His Body, the Church". Some will be motivated to preach, others to teach, others to stimulate the faith of those who are weak by coming alongside them with helpful advice and encouragement. Some will find themselves motivated perhaps in two or three directions. In addition to the gift of inspired preaching, for example, they might find themselves motivated to co-ordinate the activities of others – the gift of ruling or administration. And they might even find themselves motivated also in the direction of stimulating the faith of others.

What we must realise is that every Christian has at least one of these gifts, probably more than one, and it is only when we have an insight into this gift (or gifts) and begin to develop it (them) that we can experience true fulfilment in the Body of Christ. I said earlier that one of the main reasons for frustration amongst believers arises from the fact that many do not have an insight into their basic ministry in the Body of Christ. Joy and fulfilment come, however, when we discover our basic gift and exercise it in the way God has planned.

What happens if we fail to discover and develop our basic spiritual gift? Several things can take place: (1) *We become jealous and envious of the ministry of others.* We look at people who are functioning in the way they were designed to function, see their happiness and fulfilment and say to ourselves: "Why can't I be like them?" We forget, however, that joy comes not through copying others but by doing the thing that God has designed us to achieve (see Galatians 6:4). (2) *We become anxious and insecure.* Nothing contributes to anxiety and insecurity more than the belief "I am not sure what God wants me to do". Once we are properly engaged in doing what God planned us to do then anxiety and insecurity drop away as the leaves fall from the trees in the autumn. (3) *We become critical and judgmental in our attitudes.* Many Christians go about criticising the work of others in the Body of Christ because they feel unfulfilled in themselves. Psychology has shown us that a critical attitude often stems from a feeling of deprivation and unhappiness. We don't feel of much use ourselves and we try to compensate for it by condemning and criticising others. Once we have a positive insight into our place in Christ's Body and the function He has called us to fulfil we give no room for jealousy, insecurity, or a spirit of criticism to arise within our hearts.

Permit me, at this stage, to share with you a personal experience. I was converted to Christ at the age of 15 and, after I had been a Christian for about three years, a group of friends approached me and told me that, in their opinion, I had within me the gift of pastor (see Ephesians 4:11). "We can see it quite clearly," they said, "and we think you ought to go to a theological college and train for the ministry." I thanked them for their advice and at once wrote off to a theological college and was accepted as a candidate for the ministry. After leaving college I settled in several pastorates, all of which were greatly blessed by God. Congregations grew in numbers, the church finances increased and my friends and colleagues told me that I was a highly successful pastor. What they didn't know, however, was that inside I was deeply unhappy and greatly frustrated.

This inner frustration led in due course to a serious breakdown in my health. In fact at one point my doctors reported to my wife that they were unable to diagnose my sickness and if something dramatic did not take place within two or three days I would be dead. Well, something *dramatic* did take place. One evening whilst reading John 10:10 God broke in on my piteous condition and within a matter of minutes restored me to complete physical health. It was a miracle – one that my wife, doctors and friends joyously recognised. Following that dramatic healing I began to re-evaluate my ministry in terms of what God had fitted me to do, not so much what others thought I ought to be doing. It was during this time of reappraisal that I discovered the relevance of the three streams of gifts I have already referred to, and I began to ask myself some searching questions: "Am I really a pastor?" "Is this the ministry God has for me or has He designed me for some other purpose?" I laid aside all my preconceived ideas and came like a little child to the holy fountain of Scripture. For days I pondered and prayed over the three streams of gifts until the concept I am now sharing with you began to dawn upon me.

I saw that the first stream of gifts were gifts that we are given at our conversion, or implanted in our spirit before we were even created. My task now was to find out which of those gifts I possessed. But what about the second and third streams of gifts? What place or purpose did these have in my life? I came to realise that the gifts of the Spirit described in 1 Corinthians 12 were gifts that we are encouraged to *seek*: they are given to us as we open ourselves to the ministry of the Holy Spirit in accordance with God's sovereign purpose for our lives. The third stream of gifts, the gifts of Christ, outlined in Ephesians 4, were neither gifts we have nor gifts we should seek, but gifts we *become*. Not all Christians become pastors, teachers, evangelists, apostles, prophets: indeed only a small minority are chosen by Christ for these ministries in His Body. I saw that my problem had been that I had started out to become a pastor instead of first recognising my basic gift and then proceeding to build from there. Once I discovered and began to develop my basic gifts and sought the gifts of the Spirit that best amplified and extended my basic gifts, I found that, with no pushing or aspiration on my part, my ministry developed into that of a teacher and an evangelist. This was *confirmed by several church leaders* who witnessed in their own spirits that this was the ministry I had been designed by God to pursue.

I then resigned from the pastorate and began to pursue the ministries God had equipped me to perform. Almost immediately I discovered that I was achieving more in the Kingdom of God by doing less. Instead of minimum effectiveness with maximum weariness, it was now maximum effectiveness with minimum weariness. I had found my niche in the Body of Christ – and what a wonderful release came with this discovery.

Now I can almost hear you say: "How do I go about discovering my basic gifts? What exactly do I need to do in order to find the niche God has prepared for me?" This is the subject of the next chapter.

3

A **practical help** to gain insight into your basic gift

Before we focus on a simple but practical exercise to help us gain an insight into our basic gift or gifts, here are some important points to consider:

1. *Acquaint yourself with the meaning and purpose of each of the seven basic gifts.* Go over the list of basic gifts in Chapter 2 once again until you are sure you understand the meaning and function of each one. A jeweller who wants to deal in diamonds must acquaint himself with all kinds of gems. You will be able to identify your own gift or gifts much more easily if you take time to examine and understand each one.

2. *Approach the issue in a spirit of prayer and dedication.* When you consider that Paul's listing of the seven basic gifts in Romans 12 follows hard on the heels of his earnest appeal for every Christian to "present your bodies as a living sacrifice" it suggests we ought to approach the whole subject in an attitude of prayerful expectancy. Dedication always precedes revelation. When you dedicate your body to God as a living sacrifice then you will discover where you fit into His Body.

3. *Recognise that the following practical guide to gaining an insight into your basic gift is simply a tool and must not be overrated.* As you follow the instructions on the next page keep in mind that the statements, together with the chart on page 31, are designed to focus on the inner motivation of your spirit, or the inner drive that God has given you to function in a certain way within His Body. Such an important spiritual exercise needs further confirmation by those in your local church or fellowship. In fact, other Christians often see a gift in us long before we ourselves are aware of it. Discuss the outcome with other believers, particularly with those who know you well and who are mature Christians.

ALL GOD'S CHILDREN HAVE GIFTS

1. I enjoy presenting God's truth in an inspired and enthusiastic way.

2. I am always ready to overlook my own personal comfort in order that the needs of others may be met.

3. I find great delight in explaining the truth of a text within its context.

4. I am able to verbally encourage those who waver and are spiritually troubled.

5. I am able to manage my financial affairs efficiently so that I can give generously to the Lord's work.

6. I find it easy to delegate responsibility and organise others towards spiritual achievement.

7. I readily find myself sympathising with the misfortunes of others.

8. I am conscious of a persuasiveness of speech when encouraging people to examine their spiritual motives.

9. I have the knack of making people feel at home.

10. I delight in digging out facts concerning the Bible so that I can pass them on to others.

11. I have a deep concern to encourage people towards spiritual growth and achievement.

12. I am cheerful about giving material assets so that the Lord's work can be furthered.

13. I am able to effectively supervise the activities of others.

14. I enjoy visiting those in hospital, or the shut in's.

15. I am able to present the Word of God to a congregation of people with clarity and conviction.

16. I am happy when asked to assist others in the Lord's work, without necessarily being appointed to a leadership position.

17. I am concerned that truth should be presented in a clear fashion with proper attention to the meaning of words.

18. I am at my best when treating those who are spiritually wounded.

19. I have no problem in joyfully entrusting my assets to others for the work of the ministry.

20. I am able to plan the actions of others with ease and supply them with details which will enable them to work effectively.

21. I have a great concern for those involved in trouble.

22. I find myself preaching for a verdict whenever I present the truths of the Word of God.

23. I delight in providing a gracious haven for guests.

24. I am diligent in my study of the Bible and give careful attention to necessary research.

25. I am able to help those who need counselling over personal problems.

26. I am concerned over the question of financial assistance being available for all sections of the church.

27. I am deeply sensitive to the need of a smooth running administration so that every phase of activity is carried out decently and in order.

28. I work happily with those who are ignored by the majority.

29. I find my preaching brings people to a definite point of decision.

30. I enjoy taking the load from key people so that they can put more effort into their own particular task.

31. I am able to explain well how the Bible is a unified whole.

32. I am acutely aware of the things that hold people back in their spiritual development and long to help them overcome their problems.

33. I am careful with money and continually pray over its proper distribution in the work of the Lord.

34. I know where I am going and am able to take others with me.

35. I am able to relate to others emotionally and am quick to help when help is needed.

INSTRUCTIONS

Above are 35 statements which may help you discover your basic gift or gifts. Rate yourself using the following scale by writing the appropriate number in the corresponding number square in the chart below. Ask yourself, "Is this statement true in my spiritual life and experience?"

Greatly	3
Some	2
Little	1
Not at all	0

After you have completed the test by rating yourself for each of the 35 statements, add the scores in each horizontal row. Record the number in the Total column. Your total score for each row indicates your level of interest in that particular gift. The highest scores may lead you to a clearer understanding of the basic spiritual gift or gifts which God has deposited in your life. After you have completed the test fill in the name of each gift in the appropriate column.

						Total	Gift
A	1	8	15	22	29	_____	_____
B	2	9	16	23	30	_____	_____
C	3	10	17	24	31	_____	_____
D	4	11	18	25	32	_____	_____
E	5	12	19	26	33	_____	_____
F	6	13	20	27	34	_____	_____
G	7	14	21	28	35	_____	_____

KEY TO YOUR SPIRITUAL GIFT
Row A – Prophecy; Row B – Serving; Row C – Teaching;
Row D – Stimulating the faith of others; Row E – Giving;
Row F – Ruling or Co-ordinating; Row G – Sympathy.

Copies of this chart can be obtained for group work (in packs of 12). To order, telephone 01252 784710 for further details or visit our online store at our web site www.cwr.org.uk

Here are some additional thoughts which will help you keep the matter of discovering your basic gift in proper perspective.

The absence of any particular gift in our lives does not excuse us from obedience to clear Scriptural commands. If, for example, a person discovers they do not have the gift of "giving", they are still expected to support the Lord's work by their finances. Similarly, if a Christian finds he or she does not possess the gift of "sympathy" they are still expected to "show mercy and comfort the feeble minded" (1 Thessalonians 5:14, AV). This may raise the question in your mind: "If we are all expected to do these things then why the need for a specific gift?" The way I can best answer that question is like this: picture the Church as a football team. Every player in the team has a specific function but all are expected to try and get a goal. Each one of us has a commitment to live for Christ and to minister to each other in every way we possibly can, but God has gifted each one of us with special spiritual abilities in certain directions. This means that the enabling ministries of the Body are guaranteed and are not left to mere natural inclination. We should be watchful that the absence of a spiritual gift does not lead us into lethargy or an avoidance of our overall spiritual responsibilities.

Some Christians find it difficult to differentiate between "gifts" and "fruit" – spoken of in Galatians 5: I have often heard Christians refer to the nine qualities of the fruit of the Spirit as "gifts". They say, "I am praying for the gift of peace, or the gift of joy, or the gift of love". The fruit of the Spirit is not a gift, but the result of abiding in Christ. As our roots go down deeply into Him and we live in fellowship with Him and His Word then the fruit of the Spirit will appear in our lives by direct consequence. Each aspect of the fruit of the Spirit ought to be growing in our lives and every Christian can and should demonstrate all nine qualities of the fruit of the Spirit. Gifts, however, are distributed by the prerogative of God and one person does not possess all the gifts. To help you differentiate between "gifts" and "fruit" keep in mind that fruit has to do with character and gifts have to do with service.

Our natural abilities and aptitudes (as mentioned earlier) are often a clue to the basic spiritual gifts resident within us. John Stott, in one of his books *(God's New Society)* makes the point that the Almighty is both the God of Creation and the God of Redemption. The God who chose us before the foundation of the world (Ephesians 1:4–5) and who prepared beforehand good works for us to walk in (Ephesians 2:10) is also the God of Redemption who pours His grace upon us and endows us with spiritual gifts (Ephesians 4:7–11).

God has been sovereignly at work in our lives from the moment of conception and built into us certain abilities which He foreknew would equip us for ministry within His Body following our conversion. It stands to reason therefore that these abilities will show themselves in natural ways prior to our conversion, and after conversion become heightened and intensified to such a degree that they function in a much higher realm.

Gifts always make room for themselves. Once you discover that you have a basic gift, don't go around telling everyone, but adopt the attitude described by Paul in Philippians 2:3: "Don't be selfish; don't live to make a good impression on others. Be humble, thinking of others as better than yourself. Don't just think about your own affairs, but be interested in others, too, and in what they are doing" (TLB). Although your local church or fellowship may not at first recognise your basic gift, keep humble and prayerful and it will eventually make room for itself. The great preacher and Bible expositor of a previous generation, G.Campbell-Morgan, was rejected as a candidate for the ministry when he was 25, but his gifts eventually made room for him and he won worldwide recognition as a pastor, author and Bible teacher.

It is possible for a Christian to live for years, even a lifetime, without a consciousness of being in possession of particular basic gifts. Unused gifts really squander the grace of God. This makes the need for gaining insight into our basic gifts one of the most vital subjects in the Church as we move into the twenty-first century. Great joy flows through our lives when we exercise our basic gifts. The inner joy a person experiences in exercising a particular gift is often a clue as to its presence.

The delight and joy a person feels when ministering to others through a particular gift is communicated to those on the receiving end of that ministry and this is often reciprocated to the one ministering. This reciprocation then increases the measure of joy.

In the light of what we have said, does it not become imperative that every Christian in Christ's Body set about the task of attempting to discover and develop their basic spiritual gifts? It is only when we discover our basic gifts and seek to express them in Christ's Church that we can truly *build up* His Body.

4

The **gifts** of the **Holy Spirit** – gifts we seek

In 1 Corinthians 12:8–11 the Scripture records another set of gifts – nine in all – which are often referred to as the "Nine Gifts of the Spirit". Since the rise of the "charismatic movement" it has become popular to describe these gifts as "charismatic gifts", the thought being that unless one operates one or more of these special gifts then one is not "charismatic". The word *charisma* is derived from the Greek word *charis* which means "grace". The result of God's grace is a spiritual gift – *charisma*. In the plural form the word is *charismata* meaning the differing results of grace. Paul uses the word in his list of basic gifts in Romans 12:6: "We have different *charismata*, according to the *charis* given us ..." The word is used again in 1 Peter 4:10 where the apostle says "Each one should use whatever *charisma* he has received to serve others, faithfully administering God's *charis* in its various forms." To use the word "charismatic" of a select group of Christians is scripturally incorrect for in the Bible sense of the word *all Christians are charismatic*, as all have at least one gift.

In verse 1 of this chapter Paul uses the word *pneumatikoi* to describe the gifts. Although usually translated, "spiritual gifts", a more literal translation of the word would be "spiritual things" or "spirituals". The Greek word gives the thought of Spirit-endowed. These gifts are given and administered by the Holy Spirit for supernatural purposes and are not the result of training, experience, human insight, or prowess. If we eliminate the miraculous element from these gifts then we will miss completely the special part and place they have to play in the growth and development of Christ's Body.

In order to gain an insight into these spiritual gifts we will now proceed to examine them one by one and in the order in which they appear in the Authorised Version, the translation which, in my opinion, best brings out the truth of the Greek text.

Word of wisdom: This is not a gift of "wisdom" in a general sense, but a supernatural impartation of a fragment of God's wisdom conveyed to the mind of a believer in a crisis situation. It functions in order to enable a Christian to solve deep and complex problems which are beyond one's natural ability to solve.

Word of knowledge: Notice again it is not a gift of knowledge but a word of knowledge. This gift operates when God drops into a person's mind a fragment of His knowledge given supernaturally for a temporary and specific purpose. A classic illustration of this gift is found in Acts 5 when Peter confronted Ananias and Sapphira with the fact that they had kept back part of the purchase price of the land which they had sold. Peter had no way of knowing this apart from the knowledge which was imparted to him by the Holy Spirit. This knowledge was something he could not have gained by natural deduction but was imparted to him supernaturally by the Holy Spirit.

Faith: The Bible talks about saving faith (Ephesians 2:8–9) and many other kinds of faith, but the faith described here is *supernatural* faith – the Divinely imparted ability to believe God in an extremely difficult and perhaps dangerous situation. When it functions all human doubt is instantly dissolved and the person operating this gift speaks or acts in such a way that allows for no possible miscarriage or failure. It is, in fact, God's faith, dropped into the heart of a believer, enabling him or her to speak and act in absolute confidence that what he or she believes will come to pass.

The gifts of healing: This is the supernatural ability to bring healing to others in the power of the Holy Spirit. Notice the word here is in the plural – *gifts* of healing. This indicates that some Christians will demonstrate a gift for the healing of certain kinds of sicknesses but not for others. In my own experience, based on over fifty years in the ministry of healing, I have discovered that certain types of sicknesses and diseases respond more immediately to my own ministry of laying on of hands than do others. We might ask whether this healing is just concerned with physical healing; might it not also include emotional healing?

The working of miracles: This again is a supernatural ability given by the Holy Spirit enabling a person to perform miraculous feats. It is the releasing of the creative power of God into a dark, difficult and serious situation. I believe an example of this is seen in Acts 13:6–12 where Paul demonstrated the power to bring blindness upon Elymas the sorcerer. It is seen again in Acts 20:7–12 where the young man, named Eutychus, fell from a height and was killed. Paul ministered to him by the working of miracles (so I believe) and restored him once again to life.

Prophecy: This gift is the supernatural ability to speak spontaneously and without premeditation, a special message from God. It is quite different from the gift of prophecy in Romans 12 that we saw in Chapter 2 referred to as inspired preaching. Here the person who manifests this gift may have none of the qualities or qualifications of a preacher, yet speaks out simply and clearly the word which the Lord has given him or her.

Discerning of spirits: The gift of discerning of spirits is the supernatural ability which God gives to certain of His people to discern the motivation behind any unusual event or manifestation. There are, in the main, three sources of motivation underlying human events and activities. One flows from the Holy Spirit, another from the human spirit, and yet another from Satan himself. This gift enables a believer to pinpoint the exact source of any statement or manifestation, thus protecting the Church from counterfeits of Satan. We see this gift operating in Paul in Acts 16:16–18 when followed by a slave girl who had a "spirit by which she predicted the future". What she said was perfectly true – that "these men are servants of the Most High God" – but Paul discerned the source of that statement was Satanic. He then proceeded to cast out the evil spirit and protect the work of God from chaos and confusion.

Tongues: The gift of tongues is not linguistic ability, or a special ability given by God to learn a foreign language, but a supernatural utterance in a language never learned by the speaker. It is in fact a manifestation of the Spirit through human speech organs. There is little corporate value in this gift when used in a service unless accompanied by an interpretation, as it will be meaningless to those who are gathered.

Interpretation of tongues: This gift is the supernatural ability given by God to interpret a message that has been given in another tongue. Notice it is an "interpretation" not a "translation". In other words the person who interprets gives the *meaning* of the message and not necessarily an exact translation.

Many Bible teachers and commentators believe these gifts in 1 Corinthians 12 to be duplicates of other gifts described in the New Testament. One commentator says, for example: "The 'utterance of knowledge; and the utterance of wisdom' described in 1 Corinthians 12 is another way of describing the teaching gift which Paul later refers to in Ephesians 4:11." In my view that is a mis-statement of the situation. The gifts in 1 Corinthians 12 can operate and function alongside the gifts in Romans 12 and Ephesians 4, but they are quite distinct and separate in themselves, and operate under the control and administration of the Holy Spirit.

Once we lose sight of the fact that these gifts are supernatural in origin and operate and function miraculously under the control and direction of the Holy Spirit, we miss one of the greatest and most exciting truths of Holy Scripture. Some Christians veer away from anything to do with the supernatural. But what if we siphoned off from the Acts of the Apostles, for example, the supernatural elements in it – what would we have left? No tongues of fire! No lame man leaping for joy! No shaking of the building in which the church prayed! No piercing of the hearts of the two who attempted to deceive the church leaders! No opening of prison doors! Indeed take away the supernatural from the book of Acts (or any other part of the Bible) and you have little left. To emphasise the supernatural does not mean that we automatically devalue human learning, education or personal skills. God uses these, too. However, such are the demands made upon the Christian Church that we cannot possibly hope to meet them all unless we have access to God's supernatural and miraculous power.

Let me return now to the experience I described earlier when I set about the task of discovering my basic gifts. Once I saw that God had given me certain basic gifts I then pondered this list in 1 Corinthians 12 and asked myself, "How do these gifts relate to me?" I saw that just as God had provided me with basic abilities to do certain things well within the compass of His Church, He had also provided me, through the ministry of the Holy Spirit, with supernatural gifts that could expand and enlarge my ministry to an even greater degree than I imagined possible. I saw also that just as God had sovereignly placed within me certain basic gifts, now the Holy Spirit sovereignly wanted to supply me with the supernatural gifts which would add greatly to my effectiveness in His Body. I began to do what Paul advised, and earnestly sought the Holy Spirit for Him to express them in my life. Within months I noticed an amazing thing taking place. Having discovered that my own basic gifts were threefold – preaching, teaching and stimulating the faith of others (or personal counselling) – I began to notice that as I pursued these ministries there were times when I became conscious of some of the gifts listed in 1 Corinthians 12 being present in my life. For example, when preaching I found myself also expressing the gift of prophecy. Things I had never prepared to say flowed out from my lips and it was these things that seemed to stick in people's minds long after the rest of the sermon had been forgotten. I found, too, when counselling, that I would say to people such things as these: "Did such and such a thing happen to you when you were twelve years of age?" or "What significance do you attach to the fact that when you were eight you were sexually assaulted?" Time and time again I found myself confronting people with events I had no knowledge of and I began to realise in due course that this was the operation of the gift of the word of knowledge at work within me.

The potential for each one of our ministries when wrapped around by the supernaturalism of the Holy Spirit is beyond all telling. Once we gain an insight into our basic gifts the whole spectrum of the Spirit is open and available to us so that we can enlarge and extend our basic ministries in the Body of Christ and move forward in the direction in which God wants us to go. Many Christians, I believe attempt to force God to move in the direction they want to go, rather than first finding His basic purposes for their lives, then abandoning themselves to His purposes so that He is free to think in them, love in them and act in them the way He sees best.

5

The **gifts of Christ** –

gifts some become

aving examined the basic gifts described by Paul in Romans 12 and also the gifts of the Spirit listed in 1 Corinthians 12, it is time now to gain an insight into the gifts of the ascended Christ as seen in Ephesians 4:11–12, "And he [Christ] gave some, apostles; and some, prophets; and some, evangelists; and some, pastors and teachers; For the perfecting of the saints, for the work of the ministry, for the edifying of the body of Christ" (AV).

These five gifts are, I believe, gifted *people* who are taken by Christ and placed in His Church to accomplish specific tasks and purposes. They function in the following manner:

1. *Apostle:* The word "apostle" comes from a Greek word meaning "to send". An apostle, therefore, has a strong sense of *mission*. Some believe that the gift of apostleship was a temporary one designed mainly to establish the Church in the first few decades following the death and resurrection of Christ and when this was achieved the work and role of an apostle was no longer needed. There can be no doubt that the Twelve who were with Jesus played an unrepeatable role in the establishing of the Christian Church, but to conclude from that that the gift of

apostleship was itself temporary is to confuse the facts. Although the New Testament speaks of the Twelve as apostles in a special sense, it describes many others as apostles also. In 1 Corinthians 15 Paul differentiates between "the Twelve" (v.5) and "all the apostles" (v.7). In Galatians 1:19 and 2:9, James, the Lord's brother, is described as an apostle, yet he was not one of the Lord's disciples (see John 7:5). In Acts 14:14 and 1 Corinthians 9:5–6 Barnabas is described as an apostle. There are many other scriptures, which I do not have the space to go into here, that show many beside the Twelve exercised the gift of apostleship. But the question may be asked: "Is the ministry of apostleship a continuing ministry and is it in existence today?" I believe it is. The strongest argument for a continuing ministry of apostleship is the fact that the Scripture says this and the other four ministries in Ephesians 4 are to exist in the Church *until* we all reach unity of faith. Has that objective been reached?

What then is an "apostle" and how does he function in the Christian Church? An apostle is a person gifted by God to establish a local community of believers and assist them in laying a strong Scriptural foundation. Ideally he should be "sent out" from a church or fellowship for this express purpose, so that his ministry can be prayerfully and carefully followed. Unfortunately, many local churches in existence today have never been properly established. They came into existence as the result of an evangelistic crusade, or through a group of believers meeting together to form a local church, but because there was no ministry of apostleship present they either disintegrated or became ineffective in their structure and witness. Denominationalism I believe greatly hinders the ministry of apostleship in today's Church. There are apostles in all the evangelical denominations, who ought, in my view, to be moving through the whole Church in general, giving local churches and fellowships the benefit of their ministries, but because they stay within their denominational structures the whole Body of Christ is somewhat deprived. Many local churches need to be re-established, that is to say, they need the ministry of an apostle to come in, restructure the fellowship and help them establish clear goals for the way ahead.

2. *Prophet:* The ministry of a prophet is that of elevating the spiritual vision of the Church, to keep it up to date and to enable God's people to focus on the goals that currently God has for them. In the Authorised Version the word "prophet" appears in all three streams of gifts. It is found in Romans 12, 1 Corinthians 12 and Ephesians 4. Does this mean they are one and the same gift? No. In Romans 12, the gift (as we saw) is an inner motivation towards preaching. In Corinthians 12 it is a supernatural endowment of the Spirit by which He gives to a person the ability to speak out an unprepared word – a word for the moment. In Ephesians 4 the ascended Christ is seen as taking hold of certain individuals and fitting them into His Church with a ministry such as I have described in the definition above. Having experience of the gift of prophecy as described in 1 Corinthians 12 does not make a person a prophet in the sense of Ephesians 4. The one is a gift that functions in a local community, the other is an office which functions in a wider capacity than a local church. A prophet ideally should be moving through the whole Christian community in sharing his vision, focusing the eyes of the Body of Christ in his area (or indeed the nation) on the goals that God has for His people at that particular tune.

The main burden of a prophet's ministry is with the days immediately ahead. His predictions and conclusions, however, must always be consistent with God's written Word, the Bible, and they must always be accurate. The Scripture says, "If what a prophet proclaims in the name of the Lord does not take place or come true, that is a message the Lord has not spoken. That prophet has spoken presumptuously. Do not be afraid of him" (Deuteronomy 18:22).

A prophet is an organ of divine revelation to whom the word of the Lord is revealed. Usually the word lies in the heart of a prophet for some time before it is given, during which period the word truly becomes "flesh" in him. A prophet is not simply a communicator of words, as is someone speaking by the gift of prophecy, as in 1 Corinthians 12, but experiences the word not only in his mind but in his emotions also. As really as Christ was historically mediated to mankind through the body of Mary when the "Word became flesh" in her, so is the word of the Lord mystically mediated through the mind, the emotions and the personality of the prophet to Christ's waiting Church. He is thus able to convey not only the Word of the Lord but the *feelings* that underlie the heart of God in the issue. He speaks therefore with feeling – the feeling of God.

3. *Evangelists:* An evangelist, as listed here, is a person who is able to bring large numbers of people to personal faith in Christ. The first name to spring to mind in this connection is, of course, Billy Graham. Others are Luis Palau, Franklyn Graham, J. John, Don Double, Reinhard Bonnke – to name just a few. The men who exercise a proven ministry of bringing large numbers of people to Christ are undoubtedly, in my view, the gifts of Christ to His Church. Whilst mentioning the big names in evangelism, we ought not to overlook those who minister on a smaller scale but nevertheless are just as important. People like London City Missioners, door-to-door evangelists, and those who go from village to village preaching in small churches or tents.

It might surprise some to discover that in the other two streams of gifts there is no mention of evangelism. This is because the basic gifts of Romans 12 and supernatural gifts of 1 Corinthians 12 are for the building up of the Body, not for reaching out into the world.

Evangelism in the general sense does not flow from the reception of a specific gift but is the natural instinct of everyone who is committed to Jesus Christ. You don't need a gift to evangelise. It is true that some make more effective communicators of the Gospel because of their temperament, their training or their experience, but every single one of us is required to share our faith with our friends and acquaintances by our lips and our lives. But although every Christian is expected to be an individual witness to the Gospel of our Lord Jesus Christ, God has established in His Body a specific gift so that at certain times the Church can act corporately in sharing its faith with the world in a large meeting specifically organised for that purpose. The evangelist, it must be seen, is a gift of Christ to the Church and because of this the Church must act corporately in using these men as often as possible in presenting the claims of Christ to the whole community. Happily, whole communities of God's people, irrespective of denominations, are feeling the need to share their faith on a corporate basis, and in order for the world to see a healthy church in action evangelism must be less denominational and more inter-relational.

4. *Pastors:* Some claim that the gift of a pastor is to be combined with that of a teacher and that really we ought to be talking about one gift here, not two – a pastor-teacher. The main reasons for this view are twofold: (1) Paul designated them both by one definite article and (2) every attempt to distinguish between them in practice has proved impracticable. Although the two ministries are more closely connected than the other three we have considered, I still believe them to be separate offices within the Church. A pastor is a person who guides and guards the flock of God in a local community and gently prods them towards spiritual maturity. In other words, he is a true spiritual "shepherd". If the Church was not so inhibited by denominational structures then a pastor, in addition to his own local community, could contribute where necessary to the care of other flocks, working with the leaders of other groups (under-shepherds), adding his own spiritual insights and experience to theirs. The differences and divisions existing with the Church make it obvious that we have not arrived at the place where this kind of ministry can operate. Let us pray that one day soon it will.

5. *Teachers:* A teacher is a person gifted with the ability to make profound truths simple and has the experience to apply the principles of effective Christian living within the lives of God's people. This ministry is more peripatetic than that of a pastor and this is why I see a distinction between the two. A teacher ought to be moving amongst the Body of Christ bringing important spiritual truths to bear upon people's lives and teaching them most importantly how to resolve their problems and live effectively for Jesus Christ. The question may be asked: "What is the difference between the gift of teaching mentioned in Romans 12 and the gift of a teacher as recorded in Ephesians 4:11?" The teaching gift in Romans 12 would operate in a local community of believers (such as a house group, a Sunday School group, a youth group, etc.) where the truths of Scripture are expounded and interpreted as they relate to one's individual life. This ministry goes on in our churches week by week in a beautiful and wonderful way. God's people are taught the basics of the faith by those gifted with the ability to expound and explain the Scriptures. It so happens in church life, however, that problems emerge which need handling by men who have a deep grasp of biblical principles and are able to resolve those problems by sound systematic and clear teaching. Such a person would, in my view, be a teacher according to Ephesians 4:11.

Many years ago in South Wales, in the community where I was brought up and converted, a serious error crept into the churches which caused much heartache and distress. In almost every local church the matter was discussed by different teachers who, using their insight and experience, tried to resolve the issue on a biblical basis. This produced more division than before. Eventually, the leaders and ministers in the area decided to call in a well-known Bible teacher who, in everyone's opinion, was a teacher according to the category of Ephesians 4. Hundreds of Christians gathered together over several nights to listen to him expound the Scriptures on this particular issue that was causing concern. By the time he had finished every single person who attended the series of nightly sessions agreed that they now had the mind of the Lord on the matter. There was an instinctive reaction from the whole audience that we had witnessed the expression of one of Christ's gifts to His Church – a teacher who opened up the Scriptures on a major and vital issue that had baffled even the best minds for many months.

In almost every community of God's people there are major difficulties which crop up from time to time which need the ministry of a teacher in the Ephesians 4 category to resolve. God wants such teachers to be moving through His Church (not simply a denomination) to bring health, vitality and understanding to His Body, so that, in turn, the Body can present a unified and not a fragmented message to the world.

One question often asked whenever I speak on this subject is this: "If these three streams of gifts are the sum total of what is needed for the building up of Christ's Body, what about the other ministries in the church, such as deacons, elders, etc?" These ministries are appointed by men and not by God (see Acts 6:3). This is not to say that God is not interested in the selection of deacons or elders, or that He does not involve Himself in their appointments, but He delegates to His Church the responsibility to make these appointments, as they deem it necessary and appropriate. If a local church is sensitive to the issues I have presented in these pages, then before it appoints deacons and elders it would seek first to help the ones concerned to understand their basic gifts, for without a true understanding of this a person could be appointed to an office for which they are not ideal, or indeed suitable.

A person who does not possess the gift of "serving" would hardly make a suitable deacon and, similarly, a person who lacked the basic gifts of "ruling", "teaching" or "stimulating the faith of others" would hardly make a competent elder.

God's plan is for us to first discover and develop our basic gifts and once this is understood we should then open ourselves to the Holy Spirit so that He might endow us with the supernatural abilities that will best enlarge and amplify our basic gifts. We should never strive to go beyond this realm because if it is Christ's desire to place us in the Church as one of the gifted ministries listed in Ephesians 4, then He will do so without any pushing on our part. Remember gifts always make room for themselves. Our Lord doesn't call many to the privileged position of Ephesians 4. They are, compared to the rest of the ministries in Christ's Body, a minority stream. If it is the Master's purpose to make you an apostle, a prophet, an evangelist, a pastor, a teacher, then He will make it plain to all concerned. Nothing, nor anyone, can stop you functioning in the role that Christ has sovereignly purposed for you. If Ephesians 4:11 is where the Lord wants you to be then He will work to overcome every obstacle in your life and will confirm it not only to you but to those in leadership positions in the church or community.

The simple principle is this, when you concentrate on discovering and developing your basic gifts and open your life to the ministry of the Holy Spirit for Him to work in and through you, then the whole Trinity will determine the final outcome of your ministry. If that ministry is to be amongst the ministries of Ephesians 4.11 then God be praised. But if not, then God be praised also. The most important thing is to be what God has designed you to be; nothing less and nothing more. Joy, true joy, comes only from discovering your place in the Body of Christ *and staying in it.*

But the greatest thing ...

It should be remembered that there is one special ingredient by which all gifts must be operated. It is love. This is the binding force between all believers, without which no gift can be properly exercised or expressed. With love flowing through my heart and with a clear understanding of my place in the plan of God, how can I ever want to change place with another? As I shape my progress on this principle, I am no longer vulnerable to those who wish to impose their minds on what I should be doing for God. Once I am sure that infinite love and infinite wisdom are guiding my course, my whole being relaxes in the knowledge that God has planned the best for me, and co-operation with Him will bring my life towards His highest ideal for me – to make me like His own beloved Son.

In order to explore this theme of love more, I am including for your consideration, an insight into this most amazing chapter, 1 Corinthians 13.

The highest value – love

I'd like to name our journey over the following pages – "The Greatest Thing in the World". The title is borrowed from a spectacular sermon on 1 Corinthians 13, once preached by Professor Henry Drummond, in which he said some deeply moving things, not the least of which was this: "We have become accustomed to being told that the greatest thing in the world is faith. Well, we are wrong. Paul lists three great qualities in 1 Corinthians 13 and stands them up together – faith, hope and love. But which is the greatest? Without a moment's hesitation the decision falls – 'the greatest of these is love'."

We begin by pondering the circumstances which surround a question put to our Lord (Mark 12:28–34). What an important moment it was in the history of the universe when that lawyer stood up and asked Jesus the question: "Of all the commandments, which is the most important?"

According to Josephus, a Jewish historian, Israel had at that time more than 3,600 commandments: which one of these would Jesus choose? If he chose the wrong one, then His followers would go wrong with Him – but if He chose the right one, then his followers would go right with Him. The ages held their breath for it was a momentous moment. The future hung in the balance.

Christ went unerringly to the highest: "You must love the Lord your God with your whole heart, with your whole soul, with our whole mind, and with our whole strength ... You must love your neighbour as yourself" (Moffatt). Nothing higher can be imagined or conceived. It is the ultimate in values.

We must ask ourselves: was this emphasis unique to Jesus? Did the founder of Christianity stress something only for it to be softened by His followers? Not so. Admittedly, it appears at times that Paul, His chief interpreter, makes faith the supreme value, but when he is obliged to make a definite choice, he says: "And now these three remain: faith, hope and love. But the greatest of these is love" (1 Cor. 13:13, NIV). As one writer puts it: "Paul takes the torch from his Master's hand and holds up love as the highest and supreme value."

Peter also makes love the supreme value (1 Pet. 4:8, NIV). So for all those who follow Christ, it cannot be otherwise

So we have been saying that love is the supreme value in the Christian faith – consistently so. Scripture everywhere affirms this to be a fact, and it is the undoubted and clear verdict of the divine revelation. This poses an intriguing question: if the verdict of revelation – the truth as contained in Scripture – is that love is the supreme value of the universe, what is the verdict of those who do not believe Scripture to be infallible and do not accept it as their guide?

The surprising thing is that the scientists and psychologists of our age are increasingly agreeing that "love" is the most constructive element in the universe. Dr Carl Menninger, one of the foremost names in the field of modern-day psychiatry, wrote a book entitled, *Love Against Hate*. He took the position that the main reason why people break down is because they have not been loved and have not learned to love.

Menninger stumbled upon a principle of the universe – that love builds up and hate tears down – and many others are also coming to that conclusion. Is scientific investigation, then, leading to the same conclusion as revelation – that love is the supreme value in human nature? Inevitably so.

"God love is"

It stands to reason then, that if the greatest thing about God is the fact that He is perfect love, then the universe which He created is also designed to run on love. God has written into the universe, not only His power, but His character also. And what is His character? Simple – "God is love" (1 John 4:8). This famous text is not just telling us that God is loving. Neither is it just saying that God is lovely. It is not even saying that God has love. It is saying much more than this. The Welsh version of the Bible puts it in this way: "God love is." In other words, the reason for God's existence is love.

He does not love to exist: He exists to love. I have used the following illustration many times to explain this text – "God is love" – as it helps to clarify what John is really saying. If you take love out of an angel, what do you have left? A devil. If you take love out of a human being, what do you have left? A sinner. If you take love out of God – what do you have left? Nothing – for God is love. Love is not something God does: love is what He is.

Dr Menninger, came to the conclusion that people experience deep psychological conflicts because they have not loved or been loved. When he gained this new understanding, he called his staff together and explained that the new diagnosis demanded new treatment. He said, in essence: "These people are in our psychiatric wards because they haven't loved or been loved. So we will have to love them into loving. We will have to make all our contacts with our patients love contacts, from the top psychiatrist to the caretakers. If you go to change an electric light bulb in a patient's room, you must make your contact a love contact." They tried it for six months and found that, at the end of this period, the length of time which their patients had to spend in hospital was cut in half. Love was the key.

Another psychiatrist, Dr Smiley Blanton, came to a similar conclusion in his book, *Love or Perish*, when he said: "If you don't love, you perish – not in hell necessarily, but now as a personality. Nothing will hold the personality together except love. So love – or perish." Personally, I find it quite fascinating how some of the world's foremost social scientists are beginning to discover in their various fields the truth of what the Bible has been saying for generations – namely, that love is the highest value in the universe. Of course, they are a long way yet from seeing that the highest expression of love is love for God – but that is not discovered by scientific experimentation. Only the Holy Spirit can show them that.

All-embracing love

Bertrand Russell, the most sceptical of philosophers, said when speaking to a group of students in Columbia University, USA: "Of all the forms of caution, caution in love is perhaps the most fatal to human happiness. I see no remedy for the world's ills – except love. From various angles the necessity of love is taking the world by the hand and leading them to life's deepest necessity – love."

So then, having concluded that love is the highest value in the universe, both in God and in man, we move on now to consider how all-embracing that love is. Love is not only primary; it embraces the whole person and insists that we should love God totally and our neighbours as ourselves. Never was love defined as being so embracing and so deep as in Jesus' immortal words: "You shall love the Lord your God with all your heart, and with all your soul, and with all your mind, and with all your strength" (Mark 12:30, RSV). The call is to love God totally – the whole person is to love God wholly – no part left out. The mature and balanced person is the one who loves the Lord his God with every part of his being – the whole person wholly devoted to God. Some love God with all the strength of the mind, but are weak in other areas of their being. These are the intellectualists in Christianity – brilliant, but not very lovable. Some love God with all the strength of the soul – the affectional part of our being – but never cultivate the same degree of strength in other areas. These are the sentimentalists in Christianity – a lot of heat, but not much light.

Both types of Christians are immature. The only mature person is the one who loves the Lord his God with the strength of the heart, the strength of the soul, the strength of the mind and the strength of the body – the whole person wholly devoted to God. If you think this is a high standard, then remember that the God who demands total love is the God who gives you His total love.

It's interesting to note that the words, "with all your mind", are not included in the original commandment which God gave to Israel in Deuteronomy 6:4. Why did Jesus insert these additional words? No one can really say for sure – we can only speculate. For myself, I am grateful that Jesus added that extra phrase, for by so doing He has underlined for all time the importance of love being the controlling force of the mind.

Some years ago, when the atomic power station was built at Oak Ridge in the USA, a report stated that more people went to church in that area than in any other part of America. An observer asked the question: "Are these people more frightened?" The answer was given, "No, not frightened – reverent. They are in the presence of a great mystery – and it drives them to their knees." These people recognised that love must control the energy which modern minds have discovered, or else we shall perish – literally perish.

Jesus' statement, "You shall love the Lord your God with all your mind", stands authoritatively at the place of the greatest discovery the mind of man has made since the dawn of time – atomic energy. One of the scientists who manned the atomic station at Oak Ridge became a minister of the Gospel, and when questioned about this by the Press, gave the following reply: "I have come to see the necessity of the Christian faith, with its emphasis on love, as the controlling force in this age of atomic energy." The words, "You shall love the Lord your God with all your mind", are an up-to-the minute imperative.

At this point I must pick up once again the words of Jesus in Mark chapter 12, where He responded to an enquirer's request as to what was the greatest commandment. In answer to this request, Jesus gave a second commandment: "Love your neighbour as yourself" (v 31: NIV). If Jesus had stopped at the first and had not gone on to give the second, then humanity would have been clear about its relationship with God, but not so clear about its relationship with man. Love for God must be manifested in love to man. And Jesus added: "There is no commandment greater than these." In other words: "This is it – period."

The love we are to have towards our "neighbour" is not to be more or less than our love for ourselves, but *as* yourself. This is terribly important. It balances self-love and other-love in exact proportion.

Those who study human behaviour tell us that there are three powerful urges in our human nature – self, sex and the herd or social urge. The self urge is obviously self-regarding. The herd urge is obviously other-regarding. The sex urge is partly self-regarding and partly other-regarding.

If we accept these categories for the moment, then it means that there are two driving urges within us – self-regarding, and other-regarding. Some call them the egoistic and altruistic urges. Some organise their lives around the self-regarding urge, and become egocentric in their attitudes and actions. Such people are unhappy because they are at conflict within themselves. And why? Because the other-regarding urge is not expressed. A self-centred person is an unhappy person – in conflict with himself. Others organise their lives around the other-regarding urge, and become herd-centred people. They, too, are at war with themselves, for the self-regarding urge is unexpressed – hence frustrated. Life organised around the self is individualism. Life organised around the herd is collectivism. Both are unbalanced positions and are based on half truths, and they inevitably produce unfulfilled and unsatisfied people. Jesus steps into this conflict and offers something that meets the needs of self and the herd: "Love your neighbour [the other-regarding urge] as yourself [the self-regarding urge]." Both are balanced exactly.

James calls this principle of "loving your neighbour as yourself" the royal law. Why the "royal" law? One commentator says: "Because you belong to royalty (i.e. heaven's royalty) if you obey that law." Some Christians are greatly perplexed about this whole idea of "loving" ourselves. They say: "Are we not taught in Scripture to deny ourselves and take up our cross? Isn't 'love of self' an obnoxious weed to be uprooted from the human heart?"

In order to understand the thought we are discussing here, we must differentiate between self-love and love of self. Love of self is an obnoxious thing – narcissism. But self-love is the healthy regard one has for oneself and is, in my judgment, a necessary part of maturity. Maybe it's time to ask the Father to help you in this area.

The meaning of love

We pause now to reflect on what we mean when we use the word "love". We ask ourselves, therefore: what is the meaning of love? How do we define it? What are its ingredients and what is its true essence?

Most human definitions of love only faintly reflect – or do not reflect at all – the meaning of love as found in the New Testament. It is quite impossible to understand the meaning of love – that is, true love – unless we are prepared to look at it in relation to Jesus Christ. If we really want to understand what God and the Scriptures mean when they use the word "love", then we must see it demonstrated and exemplified in the attitudes and actions of our Lord.

It's interesting that while many of the world's great thinkers are prepared to accept that love is the highest principle in the universe, they are not prepared to link that principle to the person of Christ. They are willing to accept the principle but unwilling to accept the Person. Erich Fromm, for example, in his book *The Art of Loving*, says: "Having spoken of the love of God, I want to make it clear that I myself do not think in terms of a theistic concept, and that to me the concept of God is only a historically conditioned one, in which man has expressed his experience of his higher powers, his longing for truth and for unity at a given historical period."

Can you see what he is saying? Man puts his own content into the word "God" and is the mediator of God to himself. God, then, is all that a man sees in himself at his greatest and best moments. Those who are unwilling to take their content of the word "love" from Jesus Christ must get it from somewhere else. But from where? We either get the content of the word "love" from the Son of Man, or we have to get it from the sons of men. And what a sorry lot mankind has turned out to be! To take the principle of love and separate it from the Person who best exemplified it is to take a de-generated principle. Perhaps this is the new crucifixion of Jesus – to take His principles but reject His Person.

One of the things that intrigues me, whenever I find myself in a pre-marital counselling situation, is the answer I get from couples when I ask them how they would define the word "love". These are some of the answers I have received over the years: "Love is making your partner do what is right." "Love is giving in, rather than having a row." Norman Wright, an American marriage guidance counsellor, reports that once, when he asked a couple to define love, he got this answer: "Love is a feeling you get when you get a feeling you never felt before." A missionary told me that she was unable to use the Japanese word for love before non-Christian audiences, because it had a strong connotation of sexual love. The word had not been in contact with Jesus and was unredeemed.

Love – unconditional, unlimited

The nearest we can get to understanding the kind of love which Jesus demonstrated through His life here on earth is found in the Greek word agape. The word "agape" was in existence during the days of Christ, but it did not have the meaning then that it has now. Christians adopted the word because it was the most suitable term, giving it a distinctly Christian content. Jesus and His followers have redeemed it and filled it with divine content, so that now it carries the quality of Christ's own love which is unconditional and unlimited – a love that knows no boundaries, no restrictions, no barriers.

It is obvious that we must turn to Christian sources – to Christ – to find the true content of the word "love", and that is why I come back again to the words of Jesus: "Love one another, just as I have loved you" (John 15:12). The nearest word that we can find to describe the kind of love which Jesus exemplified when He was here on earth is the Greek word, "agape". The reason is this: that following Jesus' life, death and resurrection, Christians used the word "agape" to embody a distinctly Christian concept. With its new Christian connotation, the word stands for the most revolutionary idea ever presented to the mind of man – the idea that love is spontaneous, unmotivated and unconditional.

It's a love thing

We are ready now to lay down a Christian definition of "love", and in order to do this effectively, we must lay the two words "eros" and "agape" alongside each other.

"Eros" is acquisitive love – it longs to get; "agape" is sacrificial love – it longs to give. "Eros" is egocentric love, a form of self-assertion; "agape" is unselfish love, and seeks nothing for itself. "Eros" seeks to gain its life; "agape" lives the life of God, and therefore dares to lose it. "Eros" is the will to get and possess; "agape" is the will to distribute and dispense. "Eros" is determined by the quality, beauty and worth of its object; "agape" is sovereign in relation to its object, and is directed to both "the good and the evil". "Eros" recognises value in its object and loves it; "agape" loves and creates value in its object by the act of loving.

Do you see how clearly true love emerges from these comparisons? Here the issues are drawn. All systems and all life line themselves up on one side or the other. "Eros" loves for what it can get out of it. It turns everything – even God – into means to gain its own ends. It loves people for what they can give in return; if there is no return, then love ceases. But with "agape", the case is different. God is Agape – He is self-giving love. When Paul said, "Love never fails", he was thinking of "agape", not "eros". "Eros" love does fail – and fails very often. For at the centre of "eros" are the seeds of its own failure – it is self-seeking love.

In the light of these facts, the question you and I must ask ourselves is this: how much of my love is "eros", and how much is "agape"? The greatest danger lies, not in our being anti-Christian, but sub-Christian.

I often stand breathless before the wonder of the Father's Agape love – the Agape that came to me when I couldn't go to Him. We need to seek the Lord to help us organise our lives around "agape" love, not "eros" love – around Him, not us. And convert our "eros" into His Agape. When we get our motivations aligned with that of God the Father, then we will see the fruit of a balanced Christian "love" life.

The art of living

We now focus on a question which, when answered, will open up for us another interesting aspect of our theme. The question is this: what is the art of living? Many know everything about life except how to live it. They fail at the vital place of life – the art of living. And what is the art of living? It is simple – the art of living is loving.

A group of Bible College students once sat down during a break in their studies and asked the question: how many levels are there on which people try to live? They came up with four: (1) the level of instinct; (2) the level of duty; (3) the level of faith; and (4) the level of "faith working through love". Take the first – the level of instinct. It is impossible for humanity to live effectively on this level alone. Animals can live effectively on this level: if they respond to their physical environment by taking in food and water, they will survive, and assuming there are no great dangers facing them, spend a fairly contented existence on the earth.

Man, however, being a moral and spiritual being, is conscious of a moral as well as a physical environment – and he must respond to both if he is to live effectively on the earth. Man cannot adopt the position of an animal and say to himself: "My instincts will determine how I behave." He can say this to himself, of course, but when he tries to act on that assumption, he finds himself in trouble, for he gets tangled up in his own moral and spiritual nature and the moral universe around him. As Pascal put it: "Man is not merely a creature of instinct, but the creator of purposes."

A woman once confessed to me of her adultery with a married man. When I asked her how she felt about this, she replied: "Strangely, I feel no guilt at all." I said, "But you do realise you have committed adultery?" She replied, "Adultery is such an ugly word; I prefer to call it 'love'." I noticed that in spite of her euphemism, the moral facts were closing in upon her – she was agitated, nervous, defensive, and her conscience bore all the marks of being seared. On her knees before God she eventually sought repentance and divine forgiveness.

Love means action

Now another key question – if, as we have seen, love is such an important quality, then how do we go about the task of loving? It's easy to command, but how do we live up to that command? Can we just switch on love as we do an electric light?

When I read or heard the greatest commandment in my youth, a nagging question arose within me: how can you command love? You can command a person to do this and that, or not to do this and not to do that – but can you really command a person to love? Love, as I understand it, is an attitude that is reflected in actions, and you can hardly produce an attitude by command. Imagine a parent standing over a child, waving a big stick and saying: "Now love – or else."

John tells us that "his commands are not burdensome". On the surface of it, this statement seems somewhat contradictory. The command to love God with all our heart, all our mind, all our soul, all our strength and to love our neighbour as ourselves seems, at first sight, to be the heaviest command ever laid upon the human heart. And yet John quietly and decisively says: "His commands are not burdensome." What, then, is the answer to this seeming contradiction? Is it not this – that the God who asks us to love also provides the power to do what He commands? I do not have to love – I have to allow love to love me into loving.

In other words, the command to love does not mean that we have to reach deep down within ourselves to create feelings of love for God, but rather we should focus on how much He loves us and let His love love us into loving.

Christians who are not aware of God's fatherly, even tender love – who conceive of Him as a fearsome and frowning figure – will almost invariably have difficulty in feeling and expressing love towards God, and, for that matter, towards others also. Pascal made the point in his writings that there is no human being who will not eventually respond to love if only he can realise that he is loved. Instead of constantly reminding yourself: "I must love", focus on telling yourself: "I am loved." Then note the difference.

What is the most debilitating emotion that can distort this divine loving security? I would say without hesitation – fear. But what is fear? Many answers and definitions can be given to that question, but I believe myself that fear is basically the absence of love. When love is allowed to invade our beings, fear can have no root; when fear is allowed to invade our beings, love can have no root.

What is behind fear? This – the pain of believing that one is not loved. And nothing can cure that fear except a deep-down assurance that we are loved. This is where the Christian Gospel comes into its own, for it gives us just the assurance we need. This assurance, by the way, is not merely a verbal one – words written down in a book – but a vital one – the Word who became flesh. God became incarnate to reveal to us His love – His Agape.

Now we know that God loves us – loves us not because we are good and worthy, but because He cannot help but love. That cures our central pain – the pain of not being loved. When we get hold of this assurance and it gets hold of us, the fear of not being loved is cancelled out in our personalities, for we are loved no matter what we do or become. But it does something else, something marvellous and exciting – His love produces love in us in return.

Note however, it is not our love for Him that casts out fear, but His love for us. Have you got that? It is perfect love that drives out fear. Love – His love – begets love.

A missionary tells how, on her arrival in China many years ago, she was taken in a rickshaw through the crowded streets of the city, and as she viewed the people a wave of revulsion and horror swept over her. "O God," she cried, "how can I love these people – they are so revolting. I can't even begin to love them unless You help me." As she sat in the rickshaw, a fresh sense of how much God loved her invaded her being. She was instantly changed – and for the rest or her days, she loved them with God's love. Let us also allow the Lord to invade our hearts too.

Without love – I am nothing

We turn now to focus on one of the greatest expositions of love in the whole of literature – sacred and secular. When Dr E. Stanley Jones, the famous missionary to India, read the thirteenth chapter of First Corinthians to Mahatma Gandhi, the great leader showed evidence of deep emotion, and with tears in his eyes said: "How beautiful; how beautiful."

We cannot fully understand the opening words of 1 Corinthians 13 until we know something of the age in which Paul was writing. There were three dominant races at the time – the Greeks, the Jews and the Romans. The Greeks emphasised the power of speech and oratory; the Jews emphasised the power of the prophetic word; and the Romans emphasised the way of military might and action, being willing to sacrifice their own lives for the sake of the nation's honour.

Paul stepped into the midst of these three emphases and said: "If I speak in the tongues of men [the Greeks] and of angels, but have not love, I am only a resounding gong ... If I have the gift of prophecy [the Jews] and can fathom all mysteries and all knowledge, and if I have a faith that can move mountains, but have not love, I am nothing. If I give all I possess to the poor and surrender my body to the flames [the Romans], but have not love, I gain nothing" (vv. 1–3).

In these dramatic words of Paul, the ancient world was weighed and found wanting. A more devastating judgment was never given, for against the new more excellent way which Jesus Christ had opened up – the way of love – the lesser ways led nowhere. Paul showed in these glowing words that the future lies with love. For only love remains.

Another backdrop to Paul's letter, was the divided church of Corinth. It must have been extremely painful for the apostle to hear of the waywardness and sinful practices of some of the Corinthian Christians. Some of the things the Christians were getting involved in were deeply disappointing and disturbing, to say the least. Out of pain, however, comes a chapter that is seen by many as the greatest treatise on love ever written. One commentator says of it: "You simply cannot write such literature as this – except out of a heart of pain."

In 1 Corinthians 13, Paul spells out sixteen things about love – eight things it does do, and eight things it does not do. Love always seeks to be positive, but there are times when it has to be negative. To put no negatives in love makes love sentimental. "The negatives in love", said someone, "are the hedges along the path so that love will not stray." The first thing Paul says about love is that it is patient. Why is love patient? Because love which has a Christian content knows that in spite of the present, the future belongs to Christ. It knows that nothing wrong can come out right, and nothing right can come out wrong.

The act of patience is one thing; the attitude another. Being "kind" in the act of patience is what produces the aroma which gives it sweetness. Have you met patient people who left you unimpressed? They are patient types, but there is no "kindness" in the patience – therefore it is something less than love.

The next statement of Paul's is a negative one: "Love is not jealous, boastful or proud." Both jealousy and boastfulness show one thing – a sense of inferiority. If you are jealous of someone, you probably feel inferior to them. Boastfulness is the other side of the coin – you boast to cover up your feelings of inferiority. Pride prevents you from seeing yourself as you really are, and thus militates against true humility. The next point made by the great apostle is this: "Love is not arrogant or rude." Arrogance is something inward and need not be expressed in words. Boastfulness needs words, but arrogance does not. Arrogance is an attitude that expresses itself in rude and insulting actions. The arrogant and rude are unsure of themselves. Only the humble are sure of themselves, and only those who are sure of themselves are humble.

At the centre of these statements is another beautiful phrase: "Love does not demand its own way." The victory of love is victory over an insistent demand to have one's own way. The best way to get your own way is to surrender the desire into the hands of Christ. Then you will want not your way, but His way. When your way becomes His way, then whatever happens – you will always get your way.

Now to another characteristic of love: "Love is not irritable or resentful." The core of all resentment and irritation is an unsurrendered self. This is why it is pointless to fight resentment and irritation; instead, surrender the touchy, insecure self into Christ's hands, and the irritability and resentments will drop away. Surrender the root, and the fruit will drop away – it is no longer being fed.

Another thing love does not do is this: "Love does not rejoice at wrong, but rejoices in the right." Some Christians fall into the attitude of always looking for wrong and are disappointed when they cannot find it – especially in other Christians. What is the unconscious motive behind this? It is this: if I can find something wrong in others, then this proves my spiritual superiority, their wrongness boosts my rightness. The test of whether we are acting through love or through a desire to boost ourselves is simple: in pointing out wrong in others, do I become a more loving person? If not, then love is not the basis of my attitudes and actions. Love rejoices in the right and, by its attitudes, produces the thing it rejoices in.

Next Paul turns to focus on four positive things about love – "Love bears all things, believes all things, hopes all things, endures all things." Take the first – love bears. Why can love bear all things? Because it knows that it can use all things. Love is so powerful that is can take everything and turn it to advantage. It does with evil what Jesus did with it – turns it into good. It makes every Good Friday into an Easter Sunday.

The first and last words of Paul's statement are similar: "bears ... endures". The two central words are also similar: believes ... hopes". The two middle words save the outside words from being simply "bearing" and "enduring". Love makes bearing, not a grim, grit-your-teeth-and-never-give-up kind of bearing, but bearing with a smile. The reason why love bears and endures all things is because it has a belief and a hope that all things are being worked out according to God's eternal purposes. This saves the bearing and enduring of life's problems from being stoical, and makes it Christian. A stoic just endures things; the Christian endures – but, at the same time, exults.

"Incorrigible lovers"

The last paragraph of this famous love chapter begins with the words: "Love never fails." I remember many years ago preaching a sermon on this text to a group of young people, and afterwards, during the discussion time, the question was raised as to whether this claim of Paul's was true. The questioner said: "I have tried to show love to a boy at my school who ridicules me, scoffs at me, swears at me – but the more love I show, the worse he becomes. In my case, the love I show seems to fail."

I pointed out to him that the text did not say that love guarantees to bring about in people all the changes we would like to see, for God has made men and women with free wills, which means they are free to either receive or reject the power of love. What I believe this text means by saying that "love never fails" is that the more we love, the more loving we become, so that even if we receive no responses to our love, we have not loved in vain – we are the more loving for having loved. As Mary Reed, missionary to the lepers of the Himalayas, once put it: "Christians are such incorrigible lovers."

Paul says that prophecy will pass away, tongues will cease and knowledge will also pass away – all the gifts we have been considering in previous chapters will cease. What a death-blow these words give to many of our modern quests! To be told that our scientific achievements, our knowledge of the world's workings, our predictions of the future, our great conquests of time and space will all pass away, is to pull the rug out from under humanity's feet with a vengeance.

Of what use is our knowledge of how to split the atom unless there is love behind it to control and direct it to the good of humanity? And what use is the knowledge of how to obtain increased food crops if there is no love behind it to help the world's starving millions? Of what use is knowledge unless there is love behind that knowledge? Yes, knowledge will pass away, and only faith, hope and love will remain. And the greatest of these? Can there be any doubt? The greatest of these can be, and only ever will be – love.

Earlier in this chapter, when we were seeking to define the nature of love, we described some of the differences between the two words "eros" and "agape". E.S. Jones made this interesting comment on these two words: "The difference between 'eros' and 'agape' can never be truly understood by words – it has to be seen. Agape had to become flesh. Then, and then only, could it be known what Agape really is." How true. If Christ had not become flesh, then "agape" would have been just an interesting concept – a sweet dream. In the incarnation of Christ, however, the dream becomes a deed.

Jesus was the Word become flesh. That makes our Lord totally unique. You can't put Jesus alongside other great spiritual leaders, for they are not in the same category. They, taught – Jesus brought. And the words He spoke were part of the bringing – for His words were the revelation of His own self, every word operative within Himself. His words were deeds, and His deeds were words.

In India many years ago, a missionary spoke at a meeting which was chaired by a Hindu Member of State. The chairman said afterwards: "I could not help but contrast this meeting tonight with the meetings I attended as a boy. Then we used to heckle the missionaries and throw rotten fruit at them. But here this great audience sits in pindrop silence, listening to the Christian message. What has made the difference? Perhaps it is this: nearby is the great Miraj mission hospital where Christian doctors attend to poor and rich, night and day. Not so long ago, when I was going through a small town, I saw a lady missionary coming out of a house with her hands extended. She came up to me and said: "I'm sorry I can't shake hands with you, for my hands are plague-stained." When I saw those plague-stained hands, I saw the meaning of the Christian faith."

Through the particular – the plague-stained hands – he saw the Universal. In Jesus Christ – the Word made flesh – the Universal is made clear in the particular. His loving acts portray the highest meaning of life. When a word becomes flesh, it burns through the most resistant of materials, just as when a magnifying glass gathers up the sun's scattered rays and focuses them upon a single point.

A divine illustration

We pause to consider this thought: if "agape" love is the highest value in the universe, how could God have got us to understand that truth if He had not come to us and spelt it out in the person of His Son? Words get meaning from the life that surrounds them. A Sunday school teacher tells of how she asked a group of children who lived in a poor part of London whether they would like to go to heaven. When one of them enquired, "What's heaven like?" she replied, "It's like a home – only it's God's home." The little child said, "Then I don't want to go." To him, the word "home" meant "hell"; it took its meaning from the life that surrounded it.

It has been said that "literature can never rise higher than life" – for life puts content and meaning into literature. Suppose God had just given us the Old Testament with its beautiful descriptions of love – would that have sufficed? Hardly, for we read into words our highest experience of those words. We would see the word "love", and we would read into it our highest experience of love. But our highest experience of love is not love – at least, not love in the sense that God is love; our highest experience of love is only partial and incomplete. We tend to interpret all words according to the level of our experience.

What, then, do we need for a perfect revelation of love? We need a life to come among us – a divine life that will lift the word from the level to which we have dragged it, and put a new content into it – a divine content through a divine illustration. We would then see the word, not through what we are, but through what He is – perfect Love.

The Bible is a verbal revelation of God – the Word become words – but Christ is a vital revelation of God – the Word become flesh. You see, you cannot describe God, you can only show Him, make Him known. And Jesus is God made known in the best way He can be known – by Life. Jesus "makes known" the character of God, and makes it known in the only way character can be known – namely, through another character – His own. And the essence of that character? Unconditional love.

Jesus – mirror of the Father

We now turn to a most beautiful and intimate scripture that captures the very centre of God's loving unconditional heart for his creation. We can see how Jesus became flesh in order to show a fallen humanity the magnificence of the Father's love – a love so pure and so divine. John 1:18 is illuminated graphically in the Moffatt translation: "Nobody has ever seen God, but God has been unfolded by the divine One, the only Son, who lies upon the Father's breast." We said of this verse that Jesus, in making "God known", revealed the central thing about Him – His character. And what is the essence of His character? Eternal Love.

What a beautiful phrase Moffatt uses to describe the relationship of Christ to God: "... the only Son, who lies upon the Father's breast." The term "breast" represents the heart of God. Jesus did not come primarily to reveal the might of the Father's arm. That was part of His purpose, but not the primary one. Jesus did not come either to reveal the Father's mind. That, too, was part of His purpose – but again, not the primary one. Jesus came primarily to reveal the Father's heart – to "make known" to us that the heartbeat of our Creator is a heartbeat of love. As someone put it: "Jesus is not just in the arm of the Father – His omnipotence; nor in the mind of the Father – His omniscience. He is in the bosom of the Father – the revelation of His love."

So when Jesus came into the world, He stripped Himself of everything as He came – omnipotence (all-power), omniscience (all-knowledge), omnipresence (all-presence) – everything, that is, except love. As Charles Wesley put it in his beautiful hymn: "Emptied Himself ... of all but love" – His only protection, His only weapon, His only method.

When faced with a picture of such a sacrificial love in Jesus, I can't but see the Father also – and not in just what He says and does, but in what He is. Everything that Jesus says and does, becomes a mirror reflection of the Father – almost to the point that the two become indistinguishable – a perfect and wondrous harmony. This revelation is so wonderful that I cannot help but fall at His feet. And I wouldn't be anywhere else for all the world.

For God's sake – grow up

So let us begin to sum up what we have been saying about "The Greatest Thing in the World". Love, we said, is the supreme quality in the universe. It is the highest part of God and the highest part of man. There are different kinds of love to be seen in human relationships, but the greatest love is love that is unconditional – agape love. This love gives without thought of return. It is love par excellence.

Maturity in life – particularly the Christian life – means maturity in love. We are mature to the extent that we can love. Sometimes however, we love with the wrong kind of love – a love that is self-seeking and therefore immature. As a marriage guidance counsellor for many years, I have been driven to the conclusion that many marriages go on the rocks because one or both of the partners have not grown up – except physically. Immaturity, in fact, is high on the list of causes of marriage breakdown – immaturity in relationships, immaturity in understanding, immaturity in love. In the context in which Paul wrote to the Corinthians, it was immaturity in the use of gifts.

Immaturity in love is made evident in a number of ways. Firstly, it shows itself in being preponderantly physical. When love is weighted toward the physical – eros love – and is not held in control by spiritual love – agape – it is a fitful, immature kind of love and soon fizzles out. "Physical love is all you think of", said a disappointed wife to her husband as she tried to warn him that their marriage was heading for disaster. So it is not enough just to love – we must love with the right kind of love – agape love.

Another mark of immaturity is a demanding attitude. This kind of love is weighted towards the attitude of wanting to be loved. It is a possessive love: "I want him – or her – for myself." The emphasis here, consciously or unconsciously, is on what I can get out of it. Mature love is weighted towards self-forgetfulness and self-sacrifice. It is amazing how quickly we can distort a pure love into a selfish motivation.

I once read the story of Harold Groves, a missionary to India, who travelled from Calcutta to Bombay to visit some friends. The hosts sent their servant to the railway station to meet him, and when he asked how he might recognise the missionary, they said: "Look for a white man helping somebody – that will be him." The servant saw a white man helping an old lady step down from the train, went up to him and said: "Are you Mr Groves?" – and he was.

If you want to recognise a mature person – one who is mature in love – look for someone who is helping someone else. We are as mature as we are mature in sacrificial love. The German author, Fritz Kungel, says: "The abnormality of the child's environment may be described generally as the absence of the right kind of love." The abnormality in any environment – home, business, church – is the absence of the right kind of love – mature love. When we are mature in love, we are mature indeed.

It was said of Jesus that he "went about doing good." Some of us just "go about". We need help from the Holy Spirit to demonstrate – in our homes, our work and our church – the power of a love that is mature. We could say that we are as mature as we are mature in sacrificial love.

The high life

A while ago I came across a quotation which impressed me deeply. I am unable to trace the author, as the writer who quoted it did not give his name. Here it is: "The extent of the elevation of an animal in the scale of existence, and of course any rational being, can be infallibly measured by the degree to which sacrificial love controls that being. If there is little sacrificial love, the life is low; more sacrificial love, the life is higher; complete sacrificial love, the life is highest."

Our attitudes to life are mature or immature according to the degree of sacrificial love that is present. It is important to see, however, that what we may regard consciously as self-sacrifice may really be a device to draw attention to ourselves. I have known many Christians in my time who engaged in sacrificial service, but at the same time held an attitude of pride in the very sacrifice they were making.

That is not really self-sacrifice; it is self-aggrandisement. We push ourselves forward by pretending to hold ourselves back. Self-sacrifice is also forgetfulness of self. Years ago, I knew a Christian businessman who looked around for the biggest church in the area which offered the greatest opportunity for the sale of his goods among the members. He wanted to use the church as a basis for building up his business. His attitude was not, what can I give? but, what can I get? And that attitude, I have no hesitation in saying, is as far removed from mature love as chalk is from cheese.

Another pitfall is that it is possible also to have an immature love even while engaged in Christian work. I have met and talked to many Christians who have confessed that they have more love for the work of God than they have for God himself.

It is possible to love Christian work for the wrong reason. We may love it for what we get out of it – self-display, approval or the admiration of others. This is a strong challenge to those who are involved in Christian work, but nevertheless it is one that has to be faced. A Christian must be involved in Christian work because he loves Christ, and even if all he gets out of it is the privilege of showing his love for Christ, he should still do it joyfully and without regret.

We must be careful that we do not love the Christian cause more than we love people. I once listened to a tape of a leading minister speaking at a large conference of his denomination, in which he confessed: "In the early part of my ministry I was caught up in the thrill of the Christian cause – moving forward the Christian Church in the world. But, to my shame I admit it, I was more project-orientated than people-orientated. Projects came first – people next. God met me one day and showed me how immature was my love. I thought I was well advanced in love, but the Lord showed me that instead of advancing, I was retreating. If that interview with the Almighty had not taken place, I tremble to think where I and the church I pastor would be today." I don't wonder that this minister is sought after by many churches.

The final test

I'd like to end this chapter on "The Greatest Thing in the World" with a final challenge. To see whether your love is mature love – agape love – read 1 Corinthians 13 once again in the Revised Standard Version, replacing the word "love" in verses 4–7 with the word "I". Prepare yourself for a shock: "I am patient and kind; I am not jealous or boastful; I am not arrogant or rude. I do not insist on my own way; I am not irritable or resentful; I do not rejoice at wrong, but rejoice in the right. I bear all things, believe all things, hope all things, endure all things".

How do you come out? Are you and love identical? Our growth in maturity is a growth in that very identification. I once heard a minister ask his whole church to recite this passage together, substituting the word "we" for the word "love". He said: "If you don't honestly think our church can come up to this standard, then don't say it."

The whole group started out reciting the first line together, but as they went on scores of people dropped out. The passage was never finished, because the minister himself, after reciting just a few phrases, broke down and wept. There was no preaching that morning; instead, people fell upon their knees and asked God's forgiveness for their lack of genuine, mature love. I tell you, that meeting was the nearest I have ever been to heaven!

The context in which Paul wrote this unsurpassed description of love in 1 Corinthians 13 is that of spiritual gifts where he was seeking to address the immature love of the Corinthian church. In this book we have looked at the importance of spiritual gifts and have tried to gain insight into discovering our place in the Body of Christ, His Church. We have considered that gifts fall into three categories: basic gifts – gifts we have; gifts we seek – gifts of the Holy Spirit; and gifts some become – gifts given by Christ to build up His Church. Yet of far greater importance than the gifts is the attitude with which those gifts are used. Is it out of a self-centred "eros" love or is it from a self-giving "agape" love that is a reflection of the love of the One who is Love itself, the Lord Jesus Christ? Love was the greatest quality in His life; let it be the same in ours also.

NATIONAL DISTRIBUTORS

UK (and countries not listed below):
CWR, PO Box 230, Farnham, Surrey GU9 8XG.
Tel: 01252 784710 Outside UK (44) 1252 784710

AUSTRALIA: CMC Australasia, PO Box 519, Belmont, Victoria 3216.
Tel: (03) 5241 3288

CANADA: CMC Distribution Ltd., PO Box 7000, Niagara on the
Lake, Ontario LOS 1JO.
Tel: 1 800 325 1297

GHANA: Challenge Enterprises of Ghana, PO Box 5723, Accra.
Tel: (21) 222437/223249   Fax: 226227

INDIA: Crystal Communications, Plot No. 83, Sesachalla Society,
Entrenchment Road, East Marredpalli, Secunderabad, Andhra
Pradesh 500 026.
Tel: (40) 7732511/7730577

KENYA: Keswick Bookshop, PO Box 10242, Nairobi.
Tel: (02) 331692/226047

MALAYSIA: Salvation Book Centre (M) Sdn. Bhd., 23 Jalan SS 2/64,
47300 Petaling Jaya, Selangor.
Tel: (603) 78766411/78766797 Fax: (603) 78757066

NEW ZEALAND: CMC New Zealand Ltd., Private Bag, 17910 Green
Lane, Auckland.
Tel: 09 5249393 Fax: 09 5222137

NIGERIA: FBFM, (Every Day with Jesus), Prince's Court, 37 Ahmed
Onibudo Street, PO Box 70952, Victoria Island.
Tel: 01 2617721, 616832, 4700218, 2619156

PHILIPPINES: Praise Incorporated, 145 Panay Avenue, Cor Sgt Esguerra St, Quezon City.
Tel: 632 920 5291   Fax: 920 5747

REPUBLIC OF IRELAND: Scripture Union, 40 Talbot Street, Dublin 1.
Tel: (01) 8363764

SINGAPORE: Campus Crusade Asia Ltd., 315 Outram Road, 06–08 Tan Boon Liat Building, Singapore 169074.
Tel: (65) 222 3640

SOUTH AFRICA: Struik Christian Books (Pty Ltd), PO Box 193, Maitland 7405, Cape Town.
Tel: (021) 551 5900

SRI LANKA: Christombu Books, 27 Hospital Street, Colombo 1.
Tel: (1) 433142/328909

TANZANIA: City Christian Bookshop, PO Box 33463, Dar es Salaam.
Tel: (51) 28915

UGANDA: New Day Bookshop, PO Box 2021, Kampala.
Tel: (41) 255377

USA: CMC Distribution, PO Box 644, Lewiston, New York 14092–0644.
Tel: 1 800 325 1297

ZIMBABWE: Word of Life Books, Shop 4, Memorial Bldg., 35 S Machel Ave., Harare.
Tel: 781305   Fax: 774739

For e-mail addresses, visit the CWR web site: www.cwr.org.uk

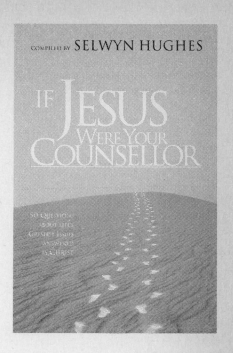

COMPILED BY SELWYN HUGHES

IF JESUS
WERE YOUR
COUNSELLOR

50 QUESTIONS
ABOUT LIFE'S
GREATER ISSUES
ANSWERED
BY CHRIST

■ If Jesus were your Counsellor

If Jesus were your Counsellor offers 50 biblical answers from the lips of Jesus to questions about faith and life. Selwyn Hughes brings more than four decades of counselling experience to this easy-to-follow and beautifully designed book which finds all its answers in *The Message* translation of God's Word. As well as being great for personal use, this book is an excellent aid to anybody involved in "people helping".

ISBN 1–85345–152–5

■ £6.95

Available from Christian bookshops or by post from National Distributors

■ Signature Series

Born to Praise and *Discovering Life's Greatest Purpose* are based on the *Every Day with Jesus* devotionals. Each lavishly designed book contains undated lessons that take just a few minutes to read each day. Daily scriptures are supported by a commentary from Selwyn Hughes, a prayer, and space for personal journal entries.

■ £6.95 each

■ In *Born to Praise* Selwyn Hughes reveals the essential tools for a life of effective worship.

ISBN 0–80542–091–6

■ *Discovering Life's Greatest Purpose* teaches us how to be sensitive to the needs of others.

ISBN 0–80542–323–0

■ *Prayer – The Greatest Power* leads us towards a deeper experience of prayer that could revolutionise our lives.

■ In *God – The Enough* Selwyn challenges us to always depend on the grace and sufficiency of God.

World-renowned

Christian Training and Resources

Ministry to Women

Counselling Training

Day and Residential Courses

Biblical Studies Courses

Regional Seminars

Books and Devotionals

Seminar Videos

Audio Cassettes

Located near Farnham in Surrey, in beautiful Waverley Abbey House, CWR have been involved in training and publishing for 35 years. Our daily devotional, *Every Day with Jesus*, is read by nearly half-a-million people around the world, and our courses in biblical studies and pastoral care and counselling are renowned for their excellence and spiritual impact. To find out more, phone the number below, write to us, or visit our web site – http://www.cwr.org.uk.

For your free brochure about our seminars and courses or a catalogue of CWR products, please phone 01252 784731 or write to:
CWR, Waverley Abbey House, Waverley Lane, Farnham, Surrey GU9 8EP.

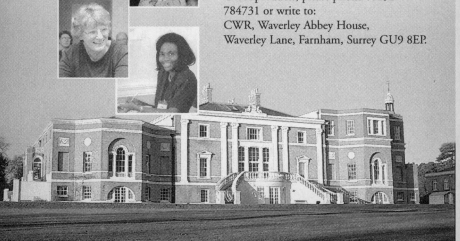